The #Buildwealth Challenge

The #Buildwealth Challenge

By Jasper Smith

LENOIR PUBLISHING

CLENOIR PUBLISHING, LLC

Published by:
C Lenoir Publishing, LLC
www.CLenoirPublishing.com
@CLenoirPublishing

This publication is designed to provide competent and reliable information regarding the subject matter covered. However, it is sold with the understanding that the author and publisher is not engaged in rendering legal, accounting, business, or other professional advice. The author is certified to render financial advice. Laws and practices often vary from state to state and if legal, financial, or other expert assistance is required, the services of a professional should be sought. The author and publisher specifically disclaim any liability that is incurred from the use or application of the contents of this book. Although the author and publisher have made every effort to ensure that the information in this book was correct at press time, the author and publisher do not assume and hereby disclaim any liability to any party for any loss, damage, or disruption caused by errors or omissions, whether errors or omissions result from negligence, accident, or any other cause.

C Lenoir Publishing, LLC books may be purchased for educational, business, or sales promotional use. For more information, permission requests, and wholesale inquiries please contact C Lenoir Publishing, LLC, at read@clenoirpublishing.com

Thank you for your support of the author's rights.

First Edition: March 2020
Book Designer: Dawn Jones x 29Eleven Media

ISBN-13: 978-0-9996116-5-4

The #Buildwealth Challenge

If you fail to plan, you plan to fail. That applies to just about anything in life and most certainly money. If you don't manage your money effectively, that spells trouble for you financially.

Many people frown at the idea of creating a financial plan. They either won't take the time to do it or will avoid meeting with a financial advisor, planner, or coach. Avoidance isn't the answer and you MUST find a way to break through whatever "it" is that's holding you back. A financial plan doesn't need to be some 100-page document, but it does need to be unique to you and your current situation. The struggle for most people is that they don't know where to start. When it comes to financial matters, people tend to over think things and make it complicated. The key is to keep things simple.

The #Buildwealth Challenge came about because of my observations on how people respond when they are challenged to do something outside of their normal routine. Whether it be a dietary challenge to eat healthier or lose weight, people tend to get behind a challenge. Sometimes it's an individual challenge to prove to yourself that you can accomplish some daunting feat, or it's you and your friends and you want to be the winner. If it's good enough for dieting or exercise, it's good enough for managing money.
Having spent my entire professional career working within the financial services sector, I understand why so many

people have issues when it comes to managing their money. Money doesn't come with instructions. Furthermore, no matter the family structure, profession, or educational background, people have issues with how to manage money. And, I finally came to the realization that money is a language; a language that many of us do not understand.

Before we kick things off, let's make sure we're on the same page. If you were going to build a house, where would you start? Start with the foundation, of course. That's what we've got to do as we learn the language of money. The goal for writing this book is simple. I must change the way you *THINK* and *FEEL* about money. If I can do those two things, you will be on your way to becoming a financial rockstar. For some, this book may serve as a reminder and will hopefully aid you in getting back on track with your financial plan. For others, this may be the start of your journey to getting your financial house in order. No matter where you fall on that continuum, after reading this book, you will have received a valuable lesson in the language of money.

Goal Setting

Any credible financial expert should start off the conversation by asking about your goals. Why is setting a goal the first step? Once a goal is identified, your attention will be focused on hitting that target.

Think about this situation. Do you know someone who told you they wanted to purchase a new car? Have you witnessed the transformation that happens as a result? This person will begin to formulate a plan and execute it flawlessly. They will identify what kind of car they want,

how much they are willing to pay for it, start saving money, and check their credit to make sure it's on point (as most people finance cars). If their credit needs a little work, they will do what it takes to clean it up. They will map out a time frame for obtaining this car and before you know it, they've got that new car.

One important thing I want you to remember, as it applies to financial goal setting, is to set a goal that's *meaningful*. I've witnessed people who bring home $2,000-$3,000/month (after taxes) and will have a savings goal of $25/month. I'm not ruling out that the person may have a variety of financial obligations, but $25 is an easy, doable amount. Why not do something more meaningful like $100 or $200? Affordability isn't the issue for that person and sometimes it's clear that people are afraid of being financially successful. Plus, we live in a consumption-focused world and it's hard to apply those larger dollars to our own financial plans. I'm certain I wouldn't have to convince someone to spend $100 or $200 on something they like to do for fun.

There isn't one specific way to handle the goal-setting process, but I support two different strategies. Whichever you decide to implement is fine.

The first strategy involves you trying to tackle:

- ***A Quick Win***
- ***A Big Win***
- ***An On-going Victory***

A quick win is a goal that you can accomplish today, tomorrow or next week. The idea is that you need something easy to accomplish first, because that will give you the courage and motivation to tackle the more challenging stuff. Once you've got a few quick wins under your belt, now you want to go after a big win.

A big win is something that you can get done in a month, 3-months, 6-months or 1 year. This win makes you feel like a champ! There may have been something that's been stressing you for a while, but you knew you needed an extended period to get it done.

Lastly, there are the on-going victories, which deal with your habits. We've all got some bad financial habits that we need to kick (or limit to some degree), and this will be the toughest thing to accomplish. My advice--slow and steady wins this race.

Here's an example. Assume you are trying to do better about managing your money and spending more wisely.

A quick win for you would be downloading a budgeting template. This is super easy to do and will take only a matter of minutes to complete. Now, you can begin to track your monthly inflows and outflows.

A big win for you could involve making the decision to stop using your credit card and work towards having your balance completely paid off in three months.

An on-going victory could involve not always jumping to purchase a flight just because an alert popped up on your phone or in your inbox. This could have been the main reason you have credit card debt— you didn't have the savings and you were using your credit card due to the fear of missing out (FOMO) on that great flight deal.

The second strategy involves setting S.M.A.R.T. goals. Here's the breakdown of the acronym:

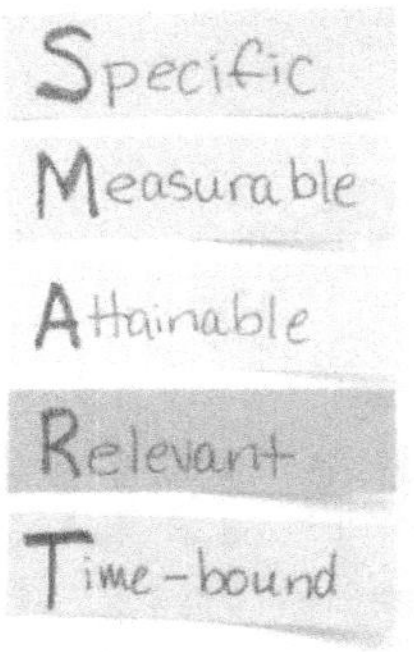

Here's an example to illustrate how this would work.

S = Save $1,200
M = Check your savings account each month to witness the increase in value
A = Yes; you can easily setup direct deposit of $100/month from your paycheck to your savings account
R = Yes; because you make plenty of money and $100/month is doable
T = One year (which breaks down to $100/month)

Don't forget, pick the strategy that suits you best. In addition to picking a strategy, write down your goals and revisit them often. Writing down your goals and revisiting them isn't a guarantee that you will achieve them, but it does improve the likelihood that you will. Therefore, written goals are your reminder that you have goals to achieve.

Let the #Buildwealth Challenge begin!!

Challenge #1

Please take a moment and circle your answer.

I track my financial progress by updating my personal balance sheet on a quarterly basis:

Disagree	**Agree**	**I have never completed a balance sheet**

You MUST take inventory before you get started! Have you ever seen those articles that report on the wealthiest man or woman in the world? Well, this is the metric they are utilizing for such reports. Before you start thinking about how you're going to #buildwealth, know how much you're worth. Also, don't feel bad if you're not making the income you desire at this point in your life. Many people judge their financial success based on how much money they make. Experience has taught me that income (while it is an important factor) is not a strong indicator of how financially successful you are. There are people who make more than $250,000/year, but when calculating their net worth, it is not a pretty sight. On the other hand, there are people who make a more modest income, like around $60,000-$70,000/year, who turn out to be extremely disciplined savers and investors.

Calculating your net worth is extremely simple to compute. Make a list of all the things that you own (your assets) and everything that you owe (your liabilities). Subtract your liabilities from your assets, thus equaling your net worth. That's it! The document that is used to calculate your net worth is called a *balance sheet.* There are some great templates that you can find on the internet, however, if you don't want to waste time searching for one, send an email to ***jasper.smith@prudential.com,*** and put "Balance Sheet" in the subject line.

Your net worth should be calculated at least on a yearly basis, which will serve as your #buildwealth barometer. However, if you feel the need to calculate it more frequently, do so twice a year or quarterly. Personally, I update my balance sheet on a quarterly basis because it keeps me in tune with my financial goals. Plus, reviewing your balance sheet frequently serves as great motivation! Everyone needs a way to measure their (financial) progress and if you can't measure something, you can't understand it. If you can't understand it, then you can't control it. And, if you can't control it, you can't improve it.

You've taken inventory, now it's time to check and make sure your money is headed in the proper direction.

Challenge #2

Please take a moment and circle your answer.

I feel like I am living check to check:

Strongly Disagree	Somewhat Disagree	Neither Agree or Disagree	Somewhat Agree	Strongly Agree

The sight of the word or hearing the word "budget" causes people to be uneasy. After you have written down your goals, the budget is the next step on the road to financial rockstar status. You've got to figure out what money is coming into your pocket and what's going out. If you don't know these numbers, stop right now, because you won't achieve your goals. YOU HAVE TO KNOW THESE NUMBERS!!!

Why do we hate budgeting so much? Especially, when we know it's the quintessential piece of our financial plan. We must commit to doing it. And, who can we blame for our budgeting woes? Is it you? Of course, it is. Your family? Yup, they had a hand in it too. The Government? You bet (I'll explain).

At some point, if YOU want to change something in your life, YOU must change! You can't just say you want to be better with your money, you must change some of your habits. It's understandable that after years and years, your habits are ingrained in you. You must slowly begin the process of breaking these harmful money habits. Stop telling yourself that you're always going to be bad with money, because you will internalize those thoughts and keep proving to yourself that you are.

Some will blame their family for their financial issues and that's perfectly fine. Most households don't have serious conversations about money. Money is a topic that many families try to avoid, yet it influences most of our decisions in life. If you grew up in a household where there was no regard for financial intelligence, you are just mimicking what they did. Please keep in mind, this doesn't just apply to money.

If you inherited poor money habits from mom and dad, you inherited a lot more! You probably inherited their eating habits, exercise habits, relationship skills, hygiene habits, and the list goes on and on. For better or for worse, your family has left a lasting impression on your life.

When the government was mentioned earlier, some of you probably asked yourself, what in the world is he talking about. Marinate on this. For as long as I can remember, anytime I've heard the government (from a federal, state or local level) discuss budgeting, three things come to mind:

1] they can't balance the budget (it's just simple math right?
2] they can't decide on what to keep in the budget and
3] they can't decide on what to take out of the budget.

Think about the psychological play that's happening. You have never witnessed "budgeting" in a positive light and there have been years upon years of negative news images, etc. around it. Don't forget, our government is made up of a group of people who struggle to get it right. Not seeing budgeting in a positive manner is certainly one of the reasons we struggle.

How exactly do we attack this budgeting fear…HEAD ON! There are hundreds of budgeting tools that exist, some in paper form, they've got a variety of apps you can download on your phone, and Microsoft Excel has numerous templates. Find the budgeting tool that suits you best because different people process things differently. If you need a budget template, send an email to ***jasper.smith@prudential.com*** and in the subject line write "Budget". I used to be terrible at budgeting until I found a strategy called the 50/20/30 plan. This plan is simple, and the simplicity is what spoke to me. I searched high and low to find the creator of this rule, but I didn't find them. Thus, I adopted the rule and made some slight alterations. The version I will share with you is the Mr. #Buildwealth version of the 50/20/30 plan.

Before we can even think about budgeting, you will need some *income*. Whether you have a 9-5 job, a part-time job or a hobby that you're turning into a legitimate business, you will need money. Consider having multiple streams of income if you truly want to #buildwealth. No matter how many sources of income that someone possesses, their money ends up in one of three areas: Essentials, Financials or Lifestyle. From all the income streams you may have, your goal is to spend no more than 50% on the *Essentials*, 20% on the *Financials* and 30% on LIFESTYLE.

50% Essentials
Shelter
Food
Utilities
Transportation

20% Financials
Savings
Debt
Insurance
Retirement
Investments

30% LIFESTYLE

Please keep in mind that this is only a framework to help you. It may be challenging to make the numbers fit perfectly, but again, we're not shooting for perfection. I just want you to see where your money is going. It is understandable that when it comes to the *Essentials* category, 50% may be challenging depending on where you reside. Personally, the first time I did this, I was at a whopping 62%! It put a ton of things in perspective for me.

Nevertheless, this framework intentionally leaves out a ton of line items, some of which you would see on normal budgeting templates. However, the idea is to change the way you *THINK* about budgeting. Consider this, focus on the 70%

(Essentials and Financials) because that's all the adult stuff you should be doing every month. That leaves you with 30% of your income to do whatever you want! That's freedom baby! This was the strategy I adopted because it put budgeting in such a positive light, and it made me *FEEL* like I could do it. And guess what, I did! After about three months of tracking with the 50/20/30, my budgeting issue ceased to exist.

Please consider using the 50/20/30 plan and let me know how things turn out.

Challenge #3

Please take a moment and circle your answer.

I currently have a monthly dollar amount that I commit to saving each month:

Strongly Disagree	**Somewhat Disagree**	**Neither Agree or Disagree**	**Somewhat Agree**	**Strongly Agree**	**I don't currently have a monthly savings goal**

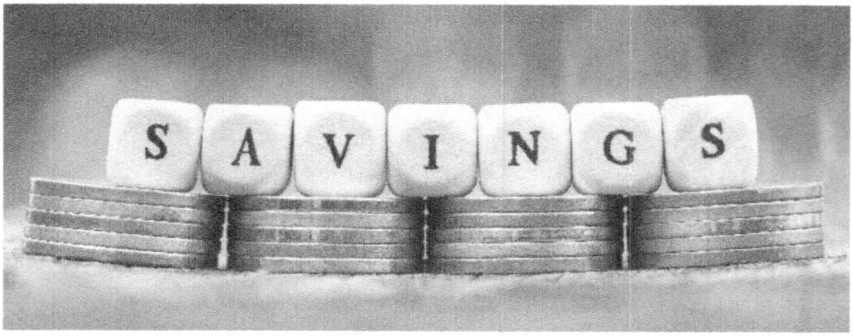

Challenge #4

Please take a moment and circle your answer.

I currently have a monthly dollar amount that I commit to investing each month:

Strongly Disagree	**Somewhat Disagree**	**Neither Agree or Disagree**	**Somewhat Agree**	**Strongly Agree**	**I don't currently have a monthly investment goal**

There isn't much to say about these last two challenges. You need to pick a dollar amount and commit to it! And yes, $1 is better than $0.

Challenge #5

Please take a moment and circle your answer.

My credit status would be classified as:

Very bad (300-560)	Bad (560- 650)	Fair (650-700)	Good (700-750)	Excellent (750-850)	I have no idea about my credit status

You may be surprised to know that many people struggle with a definition for credit. *Credit is the ability of a customer to obtain goods or services before payment, based on trust that the payment will be made in the future.* Key word in that definition…TRUST. Credit is a representation of your trustworthiness. If that definition is too wordy for you, try this out. The next time someone asks you "What is credit?" you can respond with these 3 letters O.P.M. which stands for Other People's Money. Simple right?

Why in the world is credit so important? Our US economy pretty much runs off credit. Credit is important because it reveals a lot about your character. Plus, credit affects your mortgage rates, credit card approvals, apartment requests, or it could be a determining factor when getting a job. Oh, and reviewing your credit can help you catch early signs of identity theft.

What you need to know is that there are three companies that hold a ton of power. Hopefully you've heard about these three companies…TransUnion, Equifax and Experian. You need to know what is being reported about you at each company. Some people are fans of various apps that can provide 1 or 2 of the bureau's information, but if you don't have all 3 reports, you're missing a key piece of your overall credit puzzle. Plus, when you apply for a credit card or when trying to finance a car or home, you won't know what bureau report will be pulled. I don't want you to be surprised when having your credit pulled.

Here's a good visual as it relates to the credit score. It's pretty evident, the higher the score the better.

Next, here is how your score is comprised. The diagram below displays the elements of what makes up your FICO score. There are other scoring systems, but FICO is the most popular, so that's the one we'll focus on.

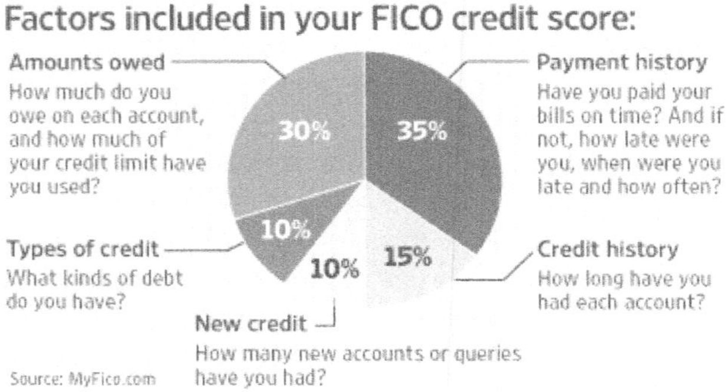

You will notice that 65% of the score is comprised of payment history and the amounts owed. When it comes to the amounts that you owe, I must debunk this myth that continues to be perpetuated in our society. You may have heard someone say "I heard it's good to carry a small balance, like 20% or 30% each month to show the bank that you're an active card user." That statement burns me up! Yes, the banks want to see the activity, but there is a huge difference between carrying a balance and being active. You carrying a balance month over month is ridiculous because you're paying the bank more money than what you owe. And, some people have the nerve to say that it's only a few dollars. Look, if I had millions of people paying me a few dollars on a monthly basis, dollars they could have avoided paying me, I would be on my personal jet somewhere flying around the world. This is how financial institutions make extra money. All those itty-bitty interest payments add up. Being active means, you borrow, you pay off the full balance, you borrow, you pay off the full balance. Make sense?

Many people may not be aware, but you have rights when it comes to credit. I won't go into detail but here's a short list of acts that you can look up when you have some free time:

Fair Credit Reporting Act (FCRA)
Fair Debt Collections Practices Act (FDCPA)
Credit Card Accountability, Responsibility and Disclosure Act (CARD)
Equal Credit Opportunity Act (ECOA)

There is one critical point that you must remember. By law, you can obtain one free credit report from each of the bureaus every 12 months. The score is not included, but if you want it, you can pay to get it. Please DO NOT pay just to see your score. If you know your credit is jacked up, why pay money just to confirm it? Get those reports and start figuring out a game plan.

Here are some negative items that could be showing on your credit report: collections, judgements, charge-offs, tax liens, and bankruptcies. You might be able to settle the account, meaning you're not going to pay back the entire balance. Here's the skinny on settling an account. If you've ever received a settlement notice from a collector (not the original company you owed), they generally give you some type of offer. It'll say something like you can settle the account for 60% of the balance. Most people think they're getting a deal, but you're not. The collection companies purchase delinquent accounts for pennies on the dollar (aka cheap). Thus, that offer still puts them in a situation to profit. You perceive to be "saving" money, but they still made a ton because they got your account for cheap. And, if you paid off the entire balance, well, they made an even bigger profit.

If settling is something you wish to pursue, keep the following in mind:

- Build a relationship with your creditors and collectors
- Make them validate the debt
- Before calling your creditor to make payment arrangements make sure you have enough money to negotiate
- The power of negotiation lies within your ability NOT to get emotional
- You have rights under the Fair Debt Collection Practices Act
- Document! Document! Document!

While settling can be good, it may still show on your report until the collector removes it. Because of that, a lender may not look at it in a favorable way. Again, your credit report tells a story. Think about this scenario. If I'm going to lend you money, and you haven't paid someone else back in full, there is a chance that once I loan you my money, you might not pay me back in full. I'm not a lender and I can't speak about what process they use to determine how they loan money. But, I think about settling in this manner. If I had 10 collection accounts and I settled 6 of them, I would *FEEL* a lot better about my situation.

If settling isn't an option you wish to pursue, you could try another technique called disputing. Under the Fair Credit Reporting Act (FCRA) you have the right to have all your information reported accurately on your credit report. You have the option to dispute information online, by phone, or by mail. You must dispute information with each of the 3 major credit bureaus: TransUnion, Equifax, and Experian.

- Dispute inaccurate information
- Report unauthorized inquiries
- Add information to your credit report
- Ask for a reinvestigation of a dispute
- Ask about not getting a response from a letter sent
- Add a Consumer Statement to your report
- Arbitrate your claims

Under the FCRA, the credit reporting agencies must respond within 30 days of receiving the letter. If the information cannot be verified as accurate or you do not receive a response, the credit-reporting agency must, by law, remove the item.

Disputing is great if you really don't have the means to pay off your collectors and your debts are old. Or, if you're just wanting to get over and try your luck, disputing could be useful. I don't have a precise time frame but from my experience, debts that are less than/equal to 2 years old have typically been verified. Verifying means they still got you on file and you're obligated to pay. And just a side note, many people dispute inaccurate information; names, bad phone numbers, wrong addresses, all of which are common occurrences on credit reports.

If you're not sure where to start, need help figuring out an attack plan, or want further assistance around the settlement or dispute process, schedule a time with me and I'll be more than happy to assist. Send an email to ***jasper.smith@prudential.com*** and write "Credit Help" in the subject line.

Challenge #6

Please take a moment and circle your answer.

I have an adequate amount of life insurance and understand the "type" of coverage I own:

Strongly Disagree	Somewhat Disagree	Neither Agree or Disagree	Somewhat Agree	Strongly Agree	I don't currently have life insurance

Life insurance is a phenomenal product, but it doesn't get the necessary love that it deserves. Many people view it only as "death insurance." I'm passionate about this product simply because I've seen way too many cases (some in my family) where there wasn't any or enough life insurance, which results in stressing the entire family. It's bad enough you've lost a loved one, and then you add financial stress to the mix. And on the flip side, I've seen a ton of instances where the family had adequate life insurance coverage and their grieving process was totally different. It's still sad you lost your loved one, but when the insurance money is there, you can take time and grieve accordingly without that added financial stress. Now, when you're ready to start taking care of business, you can proceed at the pace that makes you most comfortable.

Purchasing life insurance is a process, so let me share a few things with you about the process. My goal is to make this easy. Just follow these steps (and you MUST go in order):

Step #1: Determine how much life insurance you need?

> There is this rule of thumb that the "bread winner" in the family needs to have 8-10 times their salary in life insurance coverage [Ex: Salary = $75,000 / Life Insurance needed = $750,000] Like any rule of thumb, it's just a rule to help shape your thinking. Personally, the 8-10 times rule is a bit dated. Nonetheless, it's a great start. What you should do is connect with a life insurance agent and do a deeper dive into how much you need. Any life insurance agent can provide you with a tool or document called a Life Insurance Estimator or Life Insurance Calculator. Only after you have you completed the estimator/calculator, you will then know how much you need.

Step #2: What "type" of coverage should you purchase?

> There are two primary types of life insurance policies: *Term* and *Permanent*. To help you remember the difference between the two types of policies, here's a simple analogy. Term insurance is like renting an apartment and permanent insurance is like owning a home. Renting involves paying rent every month. Once you decide to leave, you leave without getting anything. You were simply paying money to have a roof over your head. Term insurance works similarly. By paying your (rent)

premium every month, you have coverage. However, that coverage will only last for a specified amount of time or term. For example, if you purchased a 20-year term policy, at 20 years plus one day, you would no longer have coverage. The opposite is true with permanent insurance. You pay your mortgage every month and over time, you expect your home's value to appreciate. That appreciation in your home is known as equity. The equity that builds in a permanent policy is known as cash value.

Within the term and permanent insurance categories, there are quite a few different policies. I won't go into detail of each, but no matter what policy you end up purchasing, make sure you are aware of how the policy works. Too many people have expressed to me that they were sold policies but still had questions about it. If you don't get all your questions answered, don't purchase the policy. Here's the short list of some popular types of policies you may come across:

Term [Apartment – renting]
Guaranteed Level Term Life Insurance
Annual Renewable Term Life Insurance
Return of Premium Term Life Insurance
Decreasing Term Life Insurance

Permanent [House – owning]
Whole life insurance
Variable life insurance
Universal life insurance
Variable universal life insurance
Indexed universal life insurance

After determining how much insurance is needed (step #1) you may find that you need a combination of term and permanent because of the cost. Term insurance is typically cheaper than permanent insurance. No matter which policy you select, the insurance company is going to price the policy based off two things: age and health. This process is known as underwriting. All underwriting is not created equally, and it will depend on the life insurance provider you decide to choose.

Age is a major determining factor. If you were trying to decide on whether to buy a policy now or wait five years, here's what would happen. The same exact policy is going to cost you much more five years later. Why? You're getting older which means (there's no easy way to say this) you are one year closer to leaving this earth.

Regarding your health, an insurance company wants to know what's going on with you physically. There is one exception to the health check and that involves your job. If you get life insurance through your job, you are automatically (by being an employee) given coverage. Many people tend to ask why an insurance company wants to know about your health. A life insurance company who issues a policy is 100% certain that at some point they will pay out a death benefit. But, for them to survive as a business, they need to do a thorough health check to determine the probability of how long you might live. Please keep in mind that insurance companies alone determine insurability and some people may be deemed uninsurable because of health reasons, occupation, and lifestyle choices.

As a reminder, life insurance isn't just "death insurance." Here are some alternate uses for life insurance that people don't know about:

Business planning
College planning (child policy)
Guaranteed Insurability (child policy; in case you have a family history of disease/illness)
Retirement planning

(note: Guarantees are based on the claims paying ability of the issuing company)

Challenge #7

Please take a moment and circle your answer.

I feel like I am currently on track with my current retirement plan:

Strongly Disagree	Somewhat Disagree	Neither Agree or Disagree	Somewhat Agree	Strongly Agree

I love kicking off any retirement conversation by asking someone this question: *If your retirement goal is not met would you A) Work Longer or B) Retire on less?*

I personally don't like either option, but the question forces you to choose. If you choose option A – work longer, that means you are okay sticking to your usual routine. And, you will work for however many years it takes to reach your retirement goal. You do have to hope that the work you are doing is pleasant because if you still "have to" go to work then it is important you enjoy it. If this isn't the case, you going to work every day is going to feel like serving a prison sentence. The sad reality is that there are thousands of people who HATE their jobs but are forced to tough it out because they need more money for retirement.

If option B – retire on less, is your choice, this means sacrificing "something" in the future. This sacrifice could be not taking as many trips as originally planned. Perhaps this is going to require you to move to a city where the cost of living is less. Maybe you have to scale back on all the charitable gift giving you do throughout the year. Something has got to give because you may not have extra funds to accommodate the lifestyle you initially dreamed about having.

This simple question puts things into perspective for people when it comes to retirement planning. Of course, if you don't like option A or B, hopefully, you will take your retirement plans a bit more serious and you won't have to worry about answering this question. Then, if someone were to ask you this again, your response might be something along the lines of "Oh…this question is irrelevant. I'm doing all the proper things to ensure that my retirement is going to be just the way I want it. And, I will be retiring when I'm good and ready and I will have more than enough money to truly enjoy my golden years."

Since option A and B aren't going to work, we've got to answer yet another question. *How much will you need to retire?* The answer…nobody has a freakin' clue! We don't even know what's going to happen in the next hour, let alone 20 years from now. However, there have been strides to help people focus on trying to figure out this "number." There are a few financial firms who produced a series of commercials and advertisements around trying to determine your retirement number and they did a decent job because the message was clear and simple; *your retirement number needs to be specific to you*. Most people (including me) haven't the slightest clue as to how much money is needed when they retire. Look, I'm not knocking anyone who chooses to work during their retirement years, but I think there is a HUGE difference between working because you want to and working because you have to.

Clearly, the question of how much is needed has yet to be answered. Well, there are two numbers to share. The first number is 80. Some experts have been touting that to have a glorious retirement, you need to be bringing in at least 80% of what you earn now, during your retirement years. Here's an example: If you currently earn $75,000/year, you need $60,000/year in retirement. This breaks down to $5,000/month. Some of you may say that 80% is too high, meaning you're going to be scaling back your lifestyle a bit when you retire. Others may say 80% might be too low. Again, this is one of those industry rules (and you know how I feel about these rules) that attempts to get people to focus on the importance of retirement planning.

The next number is 219. This number comes from the Rule of 219, which many of you have probably never heard of. Yes, another rule. Before we start, please be reminded that this rule makes a few assumptions. Just indulge me and let the message set in. The rule assumes there are 2 people, you and your spouse. You both retire at age 65. It is assumed that you eat 3 meals/day and each meal costs $5. You are going to do this for 20 years and there are 365 days in a year. Next, we do some multiplication: 2 x 3 x 5 x 20 x 365 = *$219,000.* If you don't have at least that much money in a retirement account, retirement is going to be tough. So, if you're reading this and you've never had a retirement goal or number in mind, shoot for having $219,000.

Now that you at least have an idea of how much you're going to need, what solutions are out there to assist you. For the sake of this book, I will not go into detail about all the bells and whistles of the various retirement accounts. However, I will provide a short list of some of the popular accounts that exist:

- Pension Plan (You're lucky if you have one because many employers have done away with these because they are expensive to maintain)
- 401k, 403b, 457b's (have a company match? DON'T MISS OUT ON THE FREE MONEY!)
- IRA's (Traditional & Roth)
- Annuities (Fixed & Variable)

Many people reading this book may be employees. If you are self-employed, you have a ton of options to consider.

Make sure to base your selection off the one that suits you and your employees best. And, if you are an employee and have one of the accounts listed above, it is highly recommended you take the time to connect with your HR/Benefits person or the retirement plan provider to ensure you have a firm understanding of your employer-sponsored retirement account.

Challenge #8

Please take a moment and circle your answer.

I am taking the proper amount of risk within my investment account(s):

Strongly Disagree	Somewhat Disagree	Neither Agree or Disagree	Somewhat Agree	Strongly Agree	I don't understand investments well enough to know how to answer this question

No matter what investment vehicle you're thinking about getting into, everything is a cycle. Look at the diagram below. This is generally what happens to most people when it comes to investing.

But what you should be doing is this...

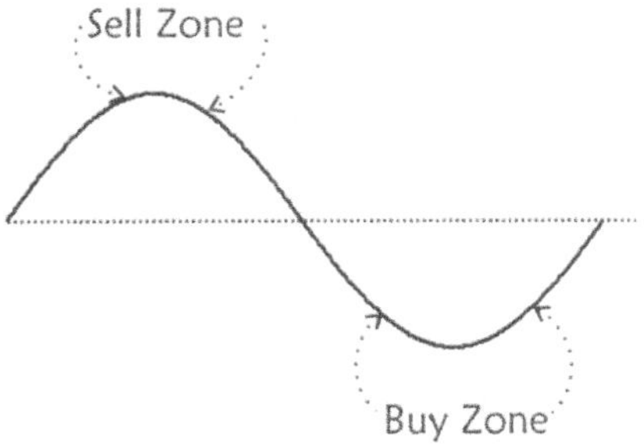

I'm sure EVERYONE is familiar with the saying "buy low, sell high." It sounds good in theory, but it's something investors continuously struggle with executing. The main issue with investing is that you never know when you're at the very top, nor will you know when things have hit their lowest point. But, that's how the game works. Only you can decide the time horizon. You've got to figure out (before you start) how long you plan on being in an investment. It is always a good time to invest in something and you will need to determine what that "something" is for you. And please, don't try to time the market. The stock market is a wild beast and if you subscribe to this practice of market timing, you will most certainly lose in the long run.

Next, you must know or understand the amount of risk that you can handle when it comes to investing. Most are familiar with the phrase "High risk, high return" and the opposite also applies "low risk, low return". Don't ever forget that because this will allow you to set expectations accordingly before you decide on a particular investment vehicle. Here's a simple diagram illustrating the various levels (tolerance) of risk.

I will focus on the two opposing ends of the risk tolerance diagram, *Very Low* and *Very High*.

For an investment that has *Very Low* risk, think bank accounts. Aside from the bank going out of business, your money is safe. If that were to happen, there is the FDIC (Federal Deposit Insurance Corporation) and the NCUA (National Credit Union Administration) insurance coverage. You can rest well at night knowing that if you went to sleep with $100 in your account, $100 would be there in the morning. In the long run, you won't make much money, but such an account is great in terms of accessibility, better known as liquidity.

Next, if we jump over to the other end of the spectrum, the *Very High* side, think about a company that just launched in a developing nation. This business could have the most revolutionary product/service. But, because it's launching in a developing nation, there may not be the infrastructure to support its business needs. Thus, this business must hope that the country begins to build that infrastructure in a timely manner, or else the company could go out of business. As each day passes, this company's primary mission is survival and, on the surface, things might not work out.

So, from an investor perspective, you might have invested a few thousand dollars, and if this company goes under, you'll probably lose everything you invested. On the flip side, if the country can sustain this company and the business has time to flourish, those initial investors who provided monetary support, will probably get a sizable return. Most people were probably betting against the company, so for those who were courageous enough to put up the money, it's only right that they get handsomely rewarded.

Here are a few other key points to remember about risk:
Your risk tolerance will change as you get more comfortable with investing. A novice investor, having no experience might find it challenging to start off very aggressive. They have no basis to make their investment decision. They may feel more comfortable starting off as a moderate investor (not playing it too safe nor too risky) until they see how the investment performs. Until they gain a better understanding, this will allow them to adjust as they see fit.

Your risk tolerance will change as you continue to earn more money or acquire more assets. How much an individual earns or the amount of assets they own, has a direct impact on that individual's risk tolerance.

For example, let's assume there are two people, you and Oprah. If you lose $50,000 on an investment that would probably destroy you. That may bother Oprah, but she would not be as nearly devastated as you because she's a billionaire.

Your risk tolerance is influenced by your time horizon. The time horizon has a huge impact on the level of risk taken. Again, think about the bank account. It makes perfect sense to have your paycheck deposited into a checking account because the funds are readily accessible to pay bills. Thus, you don't want to be risking your hard-earned paycheck. Also, as you think about retirement, it makes perfect sense to be more aggressive in your 20's because you have 30-40 years to work. You need to make sure your money is working just as hard as you do. But, as you're winding down in your career, you may need to dial it back and be more conservative because you don't have time to recoup any losses you might suffer from a downturn in the market. I cannot stress enough that you MUST know where you fall on this risk continuum as it relates to your investments.

We have reached a critical point in this investment 101 section. You have some money to invest, an idea of how the stock market goes up and down, you've examined your risk tolerance and you are ready to get started. But you may now be asking yourself two questions, (1) how do I start? and (2) what do I buy? First, make the decision as to whether to buy; stocks, bonds, mutual funds, exchange traded funds, cryptocurrency, precious metals, or real estate. There are countless things you can invest in. The idea is to do extensive research on whatever you are interested in putting your money into. Next, identify a professional (or an app) that can help with the process. You do not have to go at it alone.

The biggest challenge most people face is the fear of not knowing how an investment will perform. Or, they spend too much time doing research and never decide (called analysis paralysis). Once you've done enough research and have an idea of how things work, be courageous enough to take the plunge. There is a popular phrase you may have heard, "scared money don't make money." And if it makes you feel any better, some of the best money managers and investment experts in the world sometimes get it wrong.

The Wrap-Up

Thank you for stepping up and taking the #buildwealth challenge! Hopefully, I have shined a bright light on some key financial planning areas. This book was intended to serve as a starting point. It by no means went into deep detail on any one topic, which was intentional. Experience has taught me that most people are afraid to discuss money related matters, so I kept it light. But, as light as it is, I think anyone can grasp the concepts that were covered and apply them.

If you still aren't sure where to begin, you don't have to go at it alone. There is not a shortage of financial professionals out there. You just need to be courageous enough to reach out and let them (preferably me) know you need help. Don't worry about feeling judged or being embarrassed because you are not the only one with financial issues. Plus, once you decide to take that first (most critical) step, things get easier.

If you would like to connect and allow me to assist you with getting started with your financial plan or enhancing the one you have, drop a note to ***jasper.smith@prudential.com.***

I wish you continued success on your journey to financial rockstar status!

You don't have to go on your #buildwealth journey alone. Why not bring others along with you for the ride? Here are a few #buildwealth ideas to consider…

THINGS ARE MORE FUN WITH FAMILY

Many of us are nervous about working with a financial planner and your family members probably have the same concerns. Why not come together with your family and work on your individual financial plans as a group?

1 Round Up Your Family

Send out a text or an email to your group and see who wants to join in on this journey to financial rockstar status.

[6 people min | 10 people max]

2 Survey Your Family

Everybody has different financial concerns. You and your family will complete a brief survey to ensure we maximize the time during the group session. To get things started send an email to **jasper.smith@prudential.com**. Write ***"family"*** in the subject line and we'll send you the survey.

3 Decide Who Will Host

Someone from the group will have to decide to host the family for this session.

THINGS ARE MORE FUN WITH FRIENDS

Many of us are nervous about working with a financial planner and your friends probably have the same concerns. Why not come together with your close friends and work on your individual financial plans as a group?

1

Round Up Your Crew

Send out a text or an email to your group and see who wants to join in on this journey to financial rockstar status.

[6 people min | 10 people max]

2

Survey Your Crew

Everybody has different financial concerns. You and your crew will complete a brief survey to ensure we maximize the time during the group session. To get things started send an email to ***jasper.smith@prudential.com***. Write "***crew***" in the subject line and we'll send you the survey.

3

Decide Who Will Host

Someone from the group will have to decide to host the crew for this session.

The #BuildWealth Movement® | thebuildwealthmovement.com

THINGS ARE MORE FUN WITH CO-WORKERS

Many of us are nervous about working with a financial planner and your co-workers probably have the same concerns. Why not come together with your co-workers and work on your individual financial plans as a group?

1 Round Up Your Co-Workers

Send out a text or an email to your group and see who wants to join in on this journey to financial rockstar status.

[6 people min | 10 people max]

2 Survey Your Co-Workers

Everybody has different financial concerns. You and your co-workers will complete a brief survey to ensure we maximize the time during the group session. To get things started send an email to ***jasper.smith@prudential.com***. Write "***coworkers***" in the subject line and we'll send you the survey.

3 Decide Who Will Host

Someone from the group will have to decide to host everyone for this session.